"*Sacrament of Bodies* is a very special book. But why? Because Romeo Oriogun has developed a style that is both personal and mythical, because these poems are sensual and spiritual at once, because they give us both a story and a song, a shout and a whisper. 'I have learnt to love every broken thing,' Oriogun tells us. I find that Oriogun's tension between the high style of a sermon and the earthiness of love songs gives these poems a particularly memorable touch. It is memorable also because it is able to give us a journey (through time, through forgetting, through elegy, through exile) that is both a story of a real man in real time and an incantation, a speaking in tongues. But it is his music that finally sways me; it's music that lifts it all, that makes out of truth-telling a song. The music works here because Oriogun is a master of incantation: 'I danced,' he tells us, 'as if I knew every song had a door.' Indeed. I love this beautiful, heart-wrenching, passionate book."
—ILYA KAMINSKY, author of *Deaf Republic*

"*Sacrament of Bodies* is a gorgeous book filled with fiery pain and ecstatic desire. These poems are spacious enough to hold all the contradictions: the violence waged against gay people and the body's insistence on love, the tenderness of flesh and the carnage of war, remembering and forgetting, silence and song. Romeo Oriogun has wrought complex, elegant poems that wrench beauty from all that would kill us. As he writes, 'I worship the day because it survived the night.' I admire these poems immensely. They make me stronger."
—ELLEN BASS, author of *Indigo* and *Like a Beggar*

"In African poetry, where queer poetry still appears on the margins, *Sacrament of Bodies* harnesses the expression and truth that appeals to those of us who feel the need to shout and have raw conversations about the rights of queer people."
—TIKONDWE KAPHAGAWANI CHIMKOWOLA, *Africa in Words*

"It is inevitable that *Sacrament of Bodies* will become an influential work in contemporary poetry from Africa, especially with its centering of queer people. In Oriogun's journey, it feels like a book he needed to write. Where a weaker hand might falter under the sensitivity of such a subject, his is assured—skills he has been traversing beautifully into prose nonfiction."
—EMMANUEL ESOMNOFU, *Open Country*

"It doesn't take a reader long to be captured by Romeo Oriogun's compelling voice, a voice which seems equal parts observer, prophet, and reformer—a voice possessing the strength to rejoice amid trauma or to create visions of any ruling tyrannical force as if it were glass, to be seen through or reflected."
—JORDAN CHARLTON, *West Branch*

THE GATHERING OF BASTARDS

THE GATHERING
OF BASTARDS

Romeo Oriogun

University of Nebraska Press / Lincoln

The University of Nebraska Press is part of a land-grant institution
with campuses and programs on the past, present, and future
homelands of the Pawnee, Ponca, Otoe-Missouria, Omaha,
Dakota, Lakota, Kaw, Cheyenne, and Arapaho Peoples, as well as
those of the relocated Ho-Chunk, Sac and Fox, and Iowa Peoples.

The African Poetry Book Series is operated by the African
Poetry Book Fund. The APBF was established in 2012 with
initial support from philanthropists Laura and Robert F.
X. Sillerman. The founding director of the African Poetry
Book Fund is Kwame Dawes, Holmes University Professor
and Glenna Luschei Editor of *Prairie Schooner*.

Library of Congress Cataloging-in-Publication Data
Names: Oriogun, Romeo, author.
Title: The gathering of bastards / Romeo Oriogun.
Other titles: African poetry book series.
Description: Lincoln: University of Nebraska Press,
2023. | Series: African poetry book series
Identifiers: LCCN 2023005949
ISBN 9781496234032 (paperback)
ISBN 9781496238412 (epub)
ISBN 9781496238429 (pdf)
Subjects: LCSH: Immigrants—Poetry. | Internal migrants—
Africa—Poetry. | BISAC: POETRY / African | LCGFT: Poetry.
Classification: LCC PR9387.9.O747 G38 2023 |
DDC 821.92—dc23/eng/20230214
LC record available at https://lccn.loc.gov/2023005949

Set in Garamond Premier.

As always, for Dorcas, my mother;
and for Noura

The equilibrium you admire in me is an unstable one, difficult
to maintain. My inner life was split early between the call of
the Ancestors and the call of Europe [America], between the
exigencies of black-African culture and those of modern life.
—LEOPOLD SEDAR SENGHOR

A boat, even a wrecked and wretched boat still
has all the possibilities of moving.
—DIONNE BRAND

The relationship between earthiness and timelessness interests me a lot.
—UCHE NDUKA

CONTENTS

ACKNOWLEDGMENTS

I am grateful to the editors of the following journals and magazines, in which some of these poems have appeared or are forthcoming.

The Account: "This Way to Water," "Welcome"

Agbowo: "Assimilation"

Chicago Quarterly Review: "Wishbone"

Cincinnati Review: "Waiting for Rain"

The Common: "The Sea Dreams of Us"

Guernica: "In the Middle of August, I Saw the Sky"

Jabberwock: "A Letter from the Village of Trees"

Michigan Quarterly Review: "Nadoba"

Narrative Magazine: "Someday the Desert Will Sing," "Under the Mango Tree"

The Nation: "Late December in Abidjan"

New Yorker: "Cotonou"

Olongo Magazine: "Harmattan"

Oxford Review of Books: "All Winter I Had No Love"

Palette Poetry Journal: "Isla Verde"

Plume Poetry: "Ballet in the Cold"

Poetry: "Flyway," "Walking along Harvard Square"

Poetry London: "It Begins with Love"

Poetry Review: "From Darkness into Light," "Offerings," "On the Road to Paradise"

Prairie Schooner: "Mist"

Transition Magazine: "The World Demands from Us Our Existence"

THE GATHERING OF BASTARDS

I. DEPARTURE

Perhaps exile is us running through history

I have nothing to give, even my body is empty of a country

It Begins with Love

In the fishing village, a man whispers, *Let no body,*
bloated and gone, find its way to my boat.
He gives thanks to the wild, to the ant
running from his sandals, to the vulture standing
over the roadkill. Romeo, the day begins
with love, I tell you. After a long night,
after the rain, after the sleep of hibiscus,
the world opens its hands to sunlight.
There is time for everything, for the child
down the street struggling with his clarinet,
for the laborer kissing his wife's belly,
for the newborn seeing color. It begins
with love, I tell you, even prayers,
and I have stood in the middle of a field,
amid the gaze of antelopes. I have prayed
for thunder, a rod on my head. I, who lived
for ten months without a friend, whose sole fear
is the world so full of love, so full of loneliness,
I have panicked, wondering if to hold a drowned body
is to hold a part of myself. And from across the open
field, we hear it, a fisherman's rescue call, another body
washed out the river; we run toward it. It begins with love,
I tell you, even burial—the hand covered with sand,
a crown of seaweed. I walk to him; a song leaves me.
Omi, spare us in death, spare us in life. In the strangeness
of villages I suffer; what else is there to do?

Ballet in the Cold

after Rita Dove

Behind the rainforest we watched the stream,
its slow run through the deep cut of earth.
The night was alive, the stars burned
like little fires finding life through the dark path
filled with trees, and all around us were stalks
of wild flowers, the call of baboons, forerunners
of the ruin that awaited us.

That night death was far from us,
the day was a stranger. The gramophone
inherited from my grandpa was silent,
a dead musician teasing us from his grave.

We were naked like the day of our conception.
In the cold of the world, we sharpened our bodies
into dance, we committed ourselves into the void
of mystery. And now that the arrow of time
has been let loose into us, we must remember
that night, nature rising within us, baboons
returning to the glorious shade of trees, walking
through bush streets where the first man found fire,
iron, the brutal end of wood, devoting himself to war,
the beginning of borders, the beginning of exile.

A Letter from the Village of Trees

for Gloria

A whole year in which the fields mourn the absence
of horses, in which you sat in the open, in a country
far away from me, drinking mint tea as a projector played
Los Olvidados, Oum, So What If the Goats Die.

I was stuck in the village, living with an anthropologist
from Belgium, writing vignettes about trees, their shadows,
the swiftness of language. And on the day of the dead,
I walked away from the fellowship of the restless.

On the road that led to the river of rituals,
to the abode of those still tethered to earth,
the old men, the old workers beaten into the edge
of dust, waited by the store, waiting to order
from the bowlegged clerk, gin, rum, cigarettes
gotten from a faraway city.

The shacks between the store and Queen's Road,
made of nylon, folded and unfolded in the wind.
The language of worry was alive, shared on each door
like the blood of a firstborn lamb. And on passing
these crumbs of desolation, I saw them,

the old men, staring into distance, turning the movement
of boats into stories they will tell by moonlight;
stories of hostels forgotten at the edge of foreign cities
where men washed plates, dead bodies, old skin, and even

restrooms where a man after using a urinal spat out
his words, leaving it on the ground.

I had nothing to interpret to the world, nothing to say
to the anthropologist who walked beside me, saying,
I have studied your people and their docile ways,
their acceptance of tyrants. And as I turned to the night,
I heard the ending of a Greek play, a school boy roaring
in all seriousness into the sky, *O Ithaka, I have loved you*
through sorrow, I have loved you through the stars,
the anagram of wonder, through the vastness of the world.

Night Songs

There is something
in the air, something pushing
the wind chimes
to offer their songs. The sea
so full of life, so full
of water spirits is awake
with all the stories
like an old quilt
ready to sing of every thread
woven into it, ready to sing
a family sworn to boats. The father,
a fisherman, could at this moment
still be fishing at sea with only the moon,
a lantern for guidance, as his body
relearns the path home.

    What is the origin of anguish?
The sea
knows the secret of places.
Once, it was everywhere. Once, the sea sang
its way through the earth, a griot
with its eternal life. The griot tells me
of the fisherman still at sea.

Across time and distance, across years
and history, alone in the dark, his lullaby

enters into air as his wife stands on crossroads
            waiting for a son
                        running through cities.

The sea says, for you, this is the beginning of anguish.

Cotonou

1. THE MEETING PLACE

In some folklore birds would always meet at the edge
of a town. It was how they knew they were on a journey
to save themselves from the loss of a season.
At the intersection of three busy roads, two buses broke
down and spilled us out, humans tired of journeys.
Across the road, we watched the beauty of a palace. I smoked
and wondered how many days of sweat went into the earth
to produce such beauty. While smoking, I met a man
called Trolley, named for his expertise in flinging humans
across borders. His work of terror suffers in the coldness
of brothels across Bamako, across Tripoli, across Mauritania,
across the red sands of Kayes. He watched *his girls* drink gin
on the sidewalk. I asked him, *Do you feel shame?* He answered,
I desire beauty. In its pursuit there is no end, only ruthlessness.
The road sang a dirge, the girls danced their sadness.
There, on the road that is not home, I looked into
his eyes and saw the terror of exploitation. A leaf fell
from a tree nearby and I was reminded of the endless
movement of the world, of the girls dancing, of the sadness
of my fingers obeying the call of my body's addiction
to nicotine as a bird sang of leaving the world as it is,
a terror, a war we are still living in.

2. ADVERTISEMENT

A sign on the road read:
*Buy handmade drums and beat the wildness
of your soul.* What is the sound of all

our sorrow? Years after a war, a veteran
went crazy from hearing in his head
the wailing of a thousand women
who gave up peace to sing their dead sons
to the afterlife. Is this not a kind of wildness?
Music breeds its own fear, a sound
that leads to our loneliness like how the spools
of a cassette turning renders me into an animal
dying in an empty lair. Exile is the dying voice
of a wounded angel. I beat the drum of my life,
and the angel and I dance to the wild sadness
of life; even God ran away from this rhythm.
Look around you: we are left alone
with the mud of creation and maybe that is all
there is, the creation of a new way of life.

3. VOICES

The driver says in the night
when every passenger is asleep
he hears the true language of the road.
He says he hears the voices of cities
thousands of miles away.
The voice of exile is a murmur crossing
rivers and sea, crossing empty roads
until it washes over a man, a baptism of loss.
The driver's eyes are full of dreams,
full of the excitement of new cities.
He could be the poorer incarnate of Mansa Musa
who instead of pouring gold dust into air
pours stories to compete with sand,
stories of nomads, people running in
and out of cities. Perfect gold, this human scroll
of chronicles. Even Bessie Head, giant of letters,

who battled sands for stories, would be proud
of this precision of narrative, this perfect bridge
of imagination and the songs of mothers rocking babies
as countries cut through their bodies.

4. HOTEL DU CHIRURGIE

Our bus parked beside a water fountain
where a cherub was spilling water from pouted lips.
Across the hotel park, there were oysters
heaped on enamel trays. Fried behind walls,
they were offered to us as secrets
of the sea. Behind this market of oysters,
there was once a market for flesh,
in Ouidah, in rooms filled with Black flesh
in chains, branded like cattle, herded into pens
by other Black men paid in clear bottles of gin.
The sea crashed on naked stones
and we ran into the hotel bar.
Perched on a three-legged stool,
an old Black woman sang the fable of siblings
lost at sea; she was a lamp attracting us as moths.
Around her were opened windows, sunflowers
in broken pots. Curtains made out of beads sang
in the wind; birds flew in and out.
Smoking a carefully rolled blunt, I listened to this place;
a silent television played a Nollywood movie.
We were trapped in time, in the commodification
of flesh, saints without the gift of ablution.
In some other world, I am guilty of silence,
just as I am in this one. It was dawn
and I walked toward the bus
as the sea received into its bosom
the memory of a ship
traveling to a new world.

5. SAUDADE

While drinking coffee
on the Trans-West African Highway,
I was seized by a sadness.
I thought of roads as memories,
as dawns rising out of exile.

Collecting dust as I walked
that morning, I might be inheriting
the past, the shame of knowing
that after decades rainfall wouldn't be enough
to wash away the guilt of my ancestors.

There are moments such as this
when ancestral masks weep,
when rain bears witness to bodies
thrown overboard slave ships. Even in tears
of origin, there is no atonement enough
to restore a people lost to a ship's belly,
no forgiveness; there is only the sting
of cold air, the open Atlantic, elegy, only that.

The Wild Mystic

In the evening, walking through the paved roads of the island,
I was confronted by majestic buildings and their old names.
The cathedral where stonemasons carved their names on stones
and rejoiced in the eternal language of art was before me.

Its glory was wrapped around the figurine of a weeping Mary,
around the statue of dead angels pointing to the sea.

Around me, the island rang out like a hundred bells.

The traffic warden danced as he directed traffic.
Taxi drivers, who dreamt of old days, smoked
their Benson & Hedges, lamenting the country.

I followed the smoke of their cigarettes, turning
from the Cathedral of Christ into the long line of beggars
waiting at the entrance of a small street, jingling coins
in metal bowls, calling the world through the din
of their suffering.

There was nothing I could do to be saved, or to save
others. Powerless like a child standing before a mural,
waiting for the wall to open into the joy painted before him,
I waited, then I ran from the hallowed music of beggars.

I ran to those who loved the sea, the wind, the gospels
and their stories of hunger and bread.

In the air were the old songs of fishermen, the old songs
of frigates, the salt and music of water. There were also
the old ladies who had come to praise the blue of the sea,
its clean smell, the beauty of cracked seashells.

I, like all the others praying along the coast, had chosen
the selfishness of being, turning from the world's struggle
into the silence of faith. All around me, mystics,
with their uncombed hair, ran into water, saying hosanna
as waves washed over them.

For a while, I, too, was underwater, then it was all over.
It was nightfall, and all around me cats and stray dogs
walked like old ghosts walking to familiar places. At sea
I saw the lights of distant ships. And from afar a canoe,
lighting its way with a lantern, approached slowly, bringing
to shore the anticipation of a new day.

Wishbone

for those who died in water, drowning in history

On the way to the village, we watched
from the car as palm trees disappeared

into the past. I sat beside the coffin;
my father dressed in silk was trapped inside.

I knocked on the afterlife, once
to open the door, twice to bid him bye,

thrice to say *look at me*,
gift me the house of remembrance.

You held my head to your bosom; I smiled
for the first time. Mother, we drove past a bridge,

we watched boys dive into the allure
of water. *Here*, you said, *dead captives*

were thrown into the river. Beside the bridge
there was no stone, no marker, only canoes

tied to trees. Before us the past was a labyrinth;
I entered its mouth. No mercy lived in my fist,

only Black men, war chants in their mouths,
glistening bodies, the people they herded.

Those who died were left behind; what mercy
lives in water? What is devoured in darkness?

Here, a boy sang of air. He held a wishbone,
a dinner's remnant.

I stayed silent in history; the ropes cut through
my hands. I stayed silent in the bargaining.

30 copper bars for the men, 25 for the women,
the boy looked at me, at the rope, before being sold.

In the small hands of time, you said, *Son,*
you are not guilty. Inside of me was a hole;

within it I saw the ships, White men opening
mouths of Africans, checking teeth for decay,

writing down *stout* for those accepted,
for those staring into water.

In my mouth, the wishbone
was there. I chewed on it,

wishing it away, wishing
Black spirits rising would descend

into water. *Close your eyes,*
sprinkle salt, you said.

My father was falling into the abyss.
Hold me.

The past was rushing into my veins.
I wished nothing on the past.

I answered questions of the dead.
I am capable of terror.

Ouidah

In the house of pythons, a man met
his fear in snakes wrapped around
his neck. The man, a tourist from rural
Michigan, has come to experience *Africa*.

The man said, the task is to understand
the land, not to claim it. There's history
in the crash of waves, and in water
we are reminded, every name we know
is written in a language that came through
the arrival of ships, through the betrayal of water.

Alone in the afternoon, I wondered
if this land also called *Door of No Return*
still recognizes the sound of whips, clangs
of chains, the moment blood and sand met
on the hottest day of the year and I ran
into the coolness of water, which means
I ran into the safety of water, which means
I ran into the violence of history.

Late December in Abidjan

The city, awake and brooding, is its own thing.
I walk along Abobo; on the road everything leads
to God, even the air. I watch men spread prayer
mats, each of them full of colors like little islands.
The earth, holy in all its resurrections, moves forward,
carrying us in its silence. Away from the men,
a child leaning on a cement block tosses a ball into air
as if to say, even here, even here, I am still tender.
Yet, there is the shadow of life: the branches of trees,
leaves brittle and dry, leaning toward an unpaved road.
Loudspeakers blaring the latest song from Tanzania.
In the dance of things, the elation of life, the streets
are adorned with banners of salvation, all held together
by puppets on the outside of heaven's café. I walk
through it all, even across the carcass of a slain lamb
where a blind man led by a school boy fills his plate
with meat, saying to the world, I have traveled
through terror. Survival repeats itself again and again,
knocking on the door of every city. And before me,
a man with a stick leads a herd of Baoule cattle.
O mouth of the approaching night, we who the world
has ushered into the wildness of life are before you.
From the darkness a muezzin call. I do not understand
Arabic, but all I hear are these words. The sweet voice
of God is calling you into the private moment of the sea;
it is saying, sit, repeat your life. Like the waves

you will be led into the miracle of existence, surfing
over the small quiet heart of the world, rushing back
to where it all begins, to a slain lamb who, ribcage empty
of meat, must begin to ascend through grace.

The World Demands from Us Our Existence

So much of terror depends on movement.
I walk through the cold, across the bridge
where I visited the woman who always called
me faggot after sex, where I sat alone,
not knowing why I was there, not knowing
anything. Still, I love this life, our broken roads,
the lone bird perched on a lamp, the river
and its mystery, the earth with its village
of buried bones, all those who cried
before leaving this life. I know I will cry
when it is my turn, all the sonatas of the world
rising in me. The bird is gone, the boats too,
the river is empty, yet mercy lives in its currents
as it moves toward other cities. So much is asked of us,
I do not know why; I do not know how to choose
myself, but the birds do. I would like to join them.
I have no need for speech; I want my existence
to be a long song, a bird who after taking to air
discovers heaven is emptiness and does not lament.
Having known that there is no home apart from terror,
I lend my voice to our survival. I demand a wild life.

A Little Cartography of Violence

after the Horned Mask at the Stanley Museum, Iowa

In September when the yams were ready to depart
the darkness of the earth, I took my leave,
riding on a bus that moved toward the rugged plains
of Enugu, arriving in Udi. I arrived in the middle
of a mapmaker's dream. The hills covered with the green
foliage of our heritage shouted at the world the cardinal points
of arrival and departure. There was nothing between me
and the graves of our dead except the village below the hill,
its red earth a reminder of clay tablets, the laws of God,
the deceit of missionaries. The herd of Red Fulani cows
led down the winding road, by the whistle of a little boy,
moved like the creation of an old painter, and just before me
there was a school under a eucalyptus tree. Its teacher,
dressed in the clothes of a nun, taught the beginning
of our end, asking the students to repeat, "We were nothing
before the White man came, gifting us God, Queen, and bread."
I turned away from her language. The birds, alive
in songs, sought timelessness in this landscape of maps.
Having turned my back to the violence of language,
I stood on the peak of a hill, surveying the path of our demise,
seeing past the heads of sweet corns, seeing cities, villages,
where the British walked through, mapping the wake
of their disaster. After one hundred years, the tyranny
of memory still lives in the lines of my palms, linking me
to the shame of our fathers, shaved heads of defeat,
and when the ships left with their spoils, the maps of their *victory*,
another map was created with blood, a line drawn from the battlefield

to the stones of sacrifice where the village elders looked down
on their villages and wept. Having witnessed that this
language on my tongue will outlast our lives, I, too,
have sat on these hills and wept for our demise.

Nadoba

for those whom I cannot grieve

On our way to Nadoba, we stopped
at a restaurant in a small town.

A drunk man sang to us of sunken houses.

Striking a banjo with delicate fingers
of grief, he still sings, *Everything is dust,
even history.*

There, houses were built on the ruins
of a sunken civilization, houses were built
with love, a labor that walked walls
of reed into childhood.

When the man sings,
he is mourning his ancestors,
he is mourning his children,
he is mourning love.

To our left, we saw the anger of water,
tides swallowing roofs.

When the man sings, he is revolting
against the sea. He is beauty.

We placed coins in his palm
as we moved toward the border.

Did we pay for the beauty of grief,
or did we pay for the guilt we felt
    as he plucked his strings
and made art out of every reed wall
heavy with water, out of every drowned child?

Crossing into Togo

The Journalist says, *I have failed.*
In his palm is the guilt of exile, a pendant
made out of a rock in his birth city of Jos.

He says, *Even the voices of our people*
are dying in the river of democracy.

There are no more surprises in hearing
these stories—the madness of men weaving
havoc from statehouses has become part of our diet.

Do you want a bottle of water? I asked.

No man, no man, he kept saying.
In his words was a prison cell, an infested room
full of cockroaches, where a soldier walked in
and asked, *Where are the men you wrote about?*
Do you know them?

No man, no man, he kept saying.

Just water, I said. *Just water.*

II

A young gendarme welcomed us into the immigration office,
introduced us to a nurse who screened us for Ebola.

There, we were reminded of the cries of a people
singing that old song, which was the earth burying
her children, which was fodder for a Western camera
throwing dead Black bodies across television screens,
in airport lounges, in offices across the Atlantic.

Yet, at that border post, in the midst of those people,
some with tribal marks on their cheeks that told stories
of the first settlement of their forebears,
some with cheeks black and smooth like still water,
I was at home. Yet, I was at a border.

Passport, ID cards, come forward, 500 CFAs each to pass,
the young gendarme shouted.

Those without document stay behind, 1,000 CFAs each.

The Journalist says, *Every border is rooted into corruption;*
you have to wet the ground and continue.

The Sea Dreams of Us

Before the sea became my journey, it was love,
folktales, it was our origin staring at us,
it was our shadows, then the ships of migration
came, reminding us that years back, people left
in canoes loaded with hope, with spices, seafarers
who navigated water, holding stars in their bosoms
until the sky became road. We never saw them,
only heard the rumors, only heard that they grew wings
at the world's end, becoming ancestors, becoming
what we hear in the water at night. I am telling
this story to a girl in Accra, sitting before the sea,
watching boats named for souls who grew wings.
She laughs over a beer, saying, *I was once the day,*
I was once hope, maybe love. I have given up country
to be here, by the seaside, where what looms over me
is uncertain. I have committed no offence except
to love a man, which I know is the world's fear,
for what burns the world quicker than desire?
There is no rest in exile, there is only the road echoing
in blood, the road echoing in water, and we know it,
both of us, even when drunk: home is our breath.
The girl laughs at the sea, saying, *Our bodies are countries*
outside of borders. We watch the night, the return of boats,
the sky above Accra. The horizon beckons, the ship waits
with our journey. *What have you given up?* I ask her.
Silence is also exile, she says. We walk to the sea,
what story I carry lives in me, what story I cannot tell lives
in me. As the ship departs, I stare at it, wondering who will tell
my story; who will give me wings, who will make me fly?

Wind Whisperer

From my hotel room, just beside Noor,
Bamako spread in front of me—
a banquet of buildings,

and as always, the pigeons
native to those who hold their tongues
within language, seeking through air
the beginning—all matter and no void,
all void and the whisper of God—and as always,
they are searching for home, cooing
in the language of voyages.

Like any stranger, I had walked into this city,
the night a road, the sky a story book
I read in the tiredness of the world.

I carry within me
the sprawling slum of my childhood
as if I own my fate—but tonight, the hotel lobby
is crowded with musicians; sweet music,
tender and draining, enters my room.

The world holds me too, a soul in the waters
of the Niger. I keep drinking. I had arrived
here fully formed as desire.

And across the riverbank, the snake I met
some days ago, shedding its skin,
must still be alive somewhere.

I watched it; I saw its rebirth. Having arrived
at the end of its hunger, I knew I would do the same
and not survive. If I had known the earth is a wound
I would have begun my morning of elegies, joining
the griots to sing—*within the house of regret, there are rooms
of tenderness; sit for a while, rest, the road will still be here.*

A Village Life

All day, butterflies kept beating their wings,
moving time through light, through
the magnificent hill, in which they had found
home in the heads of wild bougainvilleas.

I watched them, sitting on a stool carved out
of an iroko, carved into the semblance of a man
grieving for a loss he cannot name.

From afar the road turned
like a wandering animal,
then it was gone.

I was left with my imagination,
I was left to think of places I could not see.

Before me was 'noon; in its busy voice
it invited everyone into the holiness of living,
it invited the woman braiding the hair
of a little girl, opening cities in her head,
offering her a glimpse of the future.

And on the dusty road, the contrite preacher
walked back and forth, a dung beetle and its curse,
carrying on his head the transgressions of our world.

The children, half naked, sat before the ever-thirsty
roots of a baobab. There is tenderness in the labor

of our lives. And in the church, under the belebo tree,
a prophetess wandered into trance, saying
to the congregation, *I am a woman weighed down
by the music of drums, a lonely woman
walking in the loneliness of an abandoned truth.*

The evening moved across the village stream,
offering gifts to those who went to fetch water,
saying to them, if noon offered you movement,
then I am offering the simplest of joy,
a time for storytelling.

And we all sat before the oldest woman, grandma
and historian. There, in the oldness of her face,
the world approached us like a decimated column,
a weakened army. Still, it marched, wearing out
the grasses, pushing us into the music of dusk.

There Is No End Here

for Dorcas

The road simply stops, then skips over houses
and fields to become part of the river,
joining the world in its quest to interpret
the purpose of our lives.

There are many questions moving along the road,
many birds circling the tree before me.

The public keeps going and coming, and in a moment
of rest, beside Dam Hotel, pigeons pick crumbs
from the sidewalk. On the hotel's balcony, there is dust
upon dust coating a chair where a man, now dead,
used to sit and watch the sun descend into water.

For a moment, I have forgotten
about my mother's death
the way cities during carnivals forget
the memories of war, pushing people through
roads till they become a blur of colors.

O stars, O night, sometimes I wonder if the dead,
in their rottenness, crack into light. I wonder
if in the sky filled with stars there is a requiem in space.

Tonight, there is nothing before me; the men come
into the hotel. I watch them dance. In the restroom,
in mirrors, the dead on my face stare back at me.

I turn away from them, walking
into the night until moonlight hits rusty roofs,
bringing me into the movement of the world.

On the Road to Paradise

after Roger Robinson

Up the grass path, littered with leftovers,
we walk. The evening is clear, the strangers
who walked in the morning have all gone;
the storks are here now. I cannot make anything of this
except the Volta River is rippling into song—a paddle
is leading it into chorus, a boatman is sitting
on the edge of his boat. I say to you: the ripples
must know our names; see how they come
toward us, eager to hug our feet, eager to hold us
like every city we have walked into. You laugh
and I remember our hotel room, the building
hidden behind tall albizzias, behind daffodils,
our room where there was no soap in the bathroom,
the bedsheet was thin, and the boy who moonlights
as a receptionist said to us, *You must be unfortunate
to find this place.* And I laughed, because we had no money,
no hope of reaching the next village. Like the winds
and floating leaves we slept beside each other.
From our bed we heard the cathedral bell, the returning
herder's voice, the mosquitoes. Now, we walk down
the river path, grasses bend underneath our feet. I yearn
to hear what they are saying, just as I yearned to hear
what you said the day we met beside the hills
but there has always been a silence in you. And I hear
the song again, the river song. I hold your hand, saying
to your palm, *This is no paradise, but it will do,
it will.* We walk down the bridge where a donkey is running
away from its cart, a farmer is running after it,

and you write into air, this is no paradise,
but we are on our way like the goose who, after surviving
an oil spill, remembered the miracle of flight
and went on its way, just like all things.
The moon is becoming bigger, the donkey and the farmer
have disappeared, we are left with his cart.
Perhaps they are building the road to paradise,
perhaps there is freedom waiting for the donkey too.

The Abandoned Church Camp

Be in permanent readiness
for the Marvelous
—Suzanne Césaire

By the river, a crow says to me, stranger,
you are so sharp with the past
like a blade
that has refused to be dulled into time.

Here, the folktale belonging to the old women
finds me weeping into freshly mowed grasses.

The sorrow of the sky is rain.
The mourners of the night are owls.

In the distance there is a reflection of the bridge
in water. It appears to me like a city.
The water ripples. The goats are fighting again;
they are fighting into the quiet sound of astonishment.

The grape in my mouth is sour.
The river is empty; it says to the riverbank,
witness the slow passing of my waters,
what you see now will be no more
in the morning hidden beyond the branches of trees.

What has sailed is arriving.
Little boats are pouring stories of Phoenicians
into air, the stories are becoming wings.

What has arrived inside of me?

I, too, have arrived at this place of rust.
The gates are open, the beds are dusty,
the spiders exhibit their ancient gossamer.
In the last light of evening, cicadas disturb the air
with the history of prayers—all those
who have knelt on this floor are alive tonight,
they are weeping into joy. You can listen
to a place from afar, but you cannot smell it.
Dear Suzanne, I am still waiting for the marvelous.

Welcome

And before dusk brought the boats home,
and before the fisherman pronounced
his great regret upon sands of Krokrobite,
I was alone, far from beachgoers,
far from Rastafari, far from the music
of salvation. Before my toes, little animals
burrowed into sand. I, too, have traveled
around the world. Boarding houses of cities,
fountains of strangers, the deep eyes
of roads have known my sleep. Before me,
the sea, wide and a stranger, held my thirst.
The rope tied to a palm tree held back
the nameless boat on sea, saying to those on board,
you will not flounder into the world of strangers.
And before dusk, the rope tugged, announcing
the fishermen's desire for home. It was time to hold
the tired beings of water, to praise trinkets around ankles
of women carrying home, to praise the fisherman's longing
for sand. I joined the long line of people pulling the boat
to shore. The sea knew our strength, it teased and let go.
What weakness we knew was a surrender to waves,
the boat rode on them. What returned was not complete,
what we held was only hope. Tomorrow we'll go out,
the sea awaits its boat. For neither grief nor pity holds
back the desire of water, the fishermen knew. And we sat,
side by side, in the makeshift store, waiting for gin, and
before us the sea continued, fast paced and ever-moving.

Migrant by the Sea

for Lolo

Why do I look upon the sea
with the awe of worship?
It is only fulfilling its duty
to the traveler and to time.
The eagle knows the fish
in water is the gateway
out of hunger. Like I knew, standing
on the seashore, the hunger
wracking a migrant's body
is movement. It is not enough
to leave home, to stare at cities
rising above the horizon. It is not
enough to migrate to the edge
of dreams. At the fireside, I talked
about cities across sea, about
the danger of crossing water.
The sea knows the names of all
it has swallowed, time knows the names
of all that have been forgotten,
yet I must dare oblivion, the quiet
despair of places, the end of blood.
If nothingness is the destination of those
drowning, if death lies at the bottom
of the sea's peace, then I have looked
into the eyes of those who have gone
before me. Now it is my turn: I must dare
the ocean; I must move into the hands of time.

The Drowned

for Lydia / for Amanda / after Derek Walcott

There is no fanfare to welcome the dead,
those who drowned at sea. There is no trumpet
blowing over the conches, over the brittle pebbles,
stringed together and worn as a necklace
by the prophet running across the beach,
allowing the wind to play music
through the shells of dead things.

That which haunted the sea, the siren
of our past, is silent. The days of miracles
are over, and the old rescue boats,
left to suffer under the unrelenting gaze
of the sea, are by the palm trees.
Alone, the boats sing for no one.
Alone, they carry forgotten journeys
within them. All they weep for, dew running down
their sides, is the rustiness of their hulls, the husk
of their dreams, the blue water at dawn
flowing like the beginning of creation
before laying the waste of the world
at the feet of this city.

There is nothing to make of it;
the sea, even with all our sorrow, will never be bitter.
Its rhythm, the last dance of the drowned,
will continue to fuel the endless coming of waves,
and before me herons and fish eagles are taking
to air. The last rescue boat at sea, named not for its resilience

but for the village drunk who goes out every night,
approaches with the dead covered in yellow tarpaulin,
and out of nowhere the air is filled with the music

of endings. And out of my mouth begins a scream,
tears, then a prayer; may I, in the evening of my life,
walk toward friends who died underwater,
in the wreck of history, singing the old songs of roads,
the music of a deer who left the dark, running toward
the only salvation he was promised: an orchard,
a turtledove calling to God, and a doe standing beside
a tree stump, gazing over the eternal field of heaven.

On Leaving

In Bobo, the roads
led to another country.
The Tuareg who fell
in love with an aid worker
was leaving for Toulouse.

His clothes sang of sand.
By the window, he read
a book in French. His shirt
read, *I have betrayed the desert*
since salt left the shores
of Morocco, since men
led slaves through the Sahara.

At dusk, he closed his book.
We were left with the elegy of places,
the silent cry of mothers, holy hour
of dua.

Outside Bobo, miles away
from Bamako, our bus, Noor,
broke down. The Tuareg invited
me and a Chadian traveling
to Dakar to the quorum
of tea drinkers. We walked
into a field, sat beside a fire,
while he boiled tea. In the sky,

stars twinkled
our eyes. The Tuareg said,

Sing, for this is what we are leaving,
for without the desert I am dead
but alive in love.

O river of my birth,
the blue depth of Ethiope,
what sorrow have you
flowed the waters into?

At the Bus Park in Bamako

In the pitiless noon, in this city made out of faith
and music, a voice from a radio announced, *I will be waiting*
in the arms of the Niger, take your time, see the world, I will be
waiting. The Park was painted white; those who sat on mats
held stories of cities, trading them among each other
for yassa, for water, for a minute phone call
to some distant lover, for a glass of lemon tea. Three boys
from Takoradi sat alone, telling everyone who walked by,
We thought this was Libya, we wanted to see the sea that bordered
Europe, we wanted to reach Lampedusa; a man brought us here,
a man abandoned us here. Every step I took was a man leaving
his country, was a man witnessing pigeons fight over leftovers,
scooters crowding the road. A man who wore an amulet,
brown leather covered with a marabout's face, boasted
of swallowing a sword. He said, *My body is like Touba,*
heavy with the bones of saints and prayers. This city that borders
history, so heavy with trade, calls to all. I wanted to hug it,
to sit in the silence of a mosque's courtyard, to sing
with the faithful, *I will be waiting, go see the world,*
I want to rest here, by a river. I want to be home, riding a scooter
to Dakar, to Thiossane, where there is soul. I am not hungry
for cities across the sea, I am not hungry for faith. Come,
come, there is a secret I must show you, something
I do not know yet, something dancing in the water
with tilapias, waiting for broken bread, for the splattering
of sunlight, for a man saying, in exile there is no revenge
against home, there is only the waiting, the slowness of light.

This Way to Water

Along Sénégal's river, in Kayes, where the bus
from Bamako dropped me off, before speeding
toward Dakar, I walk alone, trying to find
the whisper of roads, trying to sieve through water
the haunting part of home. Here, children throw stones
into water, watch them skip-skip before sinking,
a game I played as a boy. And before tall trees
whose names are lost, I stoop, picking barks,
gathering leaves, a labor to tie me to a new beginning.
I watch the rise and fall of water, the wide horizon
calling in its wisdom of ages. Here, an inlet leading
to a village speaks of possibilities. I see the women in white,
the man with his kora, playing stories of the past, suspending
history in the miracle of sound, reviving it through voices.
And the river path discovers its true purpose of worship;
the children clap. I turn from them, watching the unknown
rush toward me. Here, in the midst of women dancing
on the riverbank, I didn't discover the path
home, I only saw a goddess, the endlessness of water.

Migrant at the Sahara

Before we began the journey to Libya,
Tuaregs' falcons called the thirst
in their throats, dipping beaks in the middle
of stagnant water. The sky, opaque and dark,
was learning to be a portal. We looked
through it, we begged, *What world awaits us?*

At the outskirt of the Sahara, camels
enjoyed the softness of sand, afraid
of nothing. We watched the night
through odes, crackling fire of history.

No compass nor map, no voice
nor sword owned this place
except those christened vagabonds
by Western media, Tuaregs
whose blood mapped desert roads
we couldn't see,
guides to the edge of the continent.

They cried, *Fill your thirst, tie your lives
to your hearts.* We listened. The trucks
were there, death too, at least its echo.
We leaned toward the light of dawn;
our bodies prayed for passage through
sands where death was a whitened bone.
Before a mosque, the last tracks of yesterday's
trucks stood before winds, waiting to be erased
by the next journey. Afraid of death, I turned back.

Someday the Desert Will Sing

after Tade Ipadeola

On the day of equinox, the camels walk slowly,
neither responding to the voice of their herders
or to the dunes slowly shifting through an endless arena
of sand. In the Sahara, where water is an old tale
and the herders and the animals are one, united in life
as well as in an ongoing battle toward death,
there is a beginning in every grain of sand,
there is an origin in the night wind,
and the caves with their many moments of history
hold all that we need to speak from. Of death
they have seen its skeleton; they have held its endless
echo. Of life they have seen the nighttime dew,
the shepherd's garment, the dog lying down on the thigh
of a lost stranger, the plants finding strength
in darkness. What speaks in the wind is the endless march
of migrants, the Bedouins and their singing moon,
the Nubian ibex's stubbornness, old tracks
of Arab traders bridging West Africa and the Mediterranean
through bags of salts, then jihads, then the movement
of slaves. Through all of this the sands kept vigil,
harboring blood and bones, harboring the beauty
of the rising sun between seven dunes. A Berber
I met in Bamako said, *When the rebab sings*
its strings belong to the desert, it tells the story
of falling stars, of the sands. Listen, he said,
just before the song of the rebab becomes the voice
of God you will hear the sound of trickling sand,
the history of movement, which is the history of life,

then death. Someday when you belong to the sands
you will know the desert's voyage toward the sea,
its calligraphy of the world, its return to a cave
where a shepherd sings of the city, "All your buildings
pale before sunrays moving away from the desert;
all your beauty is silent, waiting for the desert
to speak into the night, to speak even the secret of water."

Ait-Ben-Haddou

The wind was merciful to the traveler who wandered
at dawn into an abandoned city.

He counted the forts, mosques, the pillars
that knew the hands of children resting on them.

He laughed, this wanderer who heard of this city
during his desert sojourn, who heard the story
of a wounded soldier fleeing from battle, banging
on its metal gates until sanctuary was opened to him.
Under an olive tree the wounded soldier drank water,
offered his thanks to the women dressing his wounds
as he listened to children reciting the Koran,
to butchers haggling with city wives over meat,
to fat dogs running between tables, barking,
snatching offal, to men covered in dust
teaching young boys how to map rain.

After he'd rested, the soldier went back to battle,
carrying with him the hope of his city.

The wanderer laughed at history, saying to himself,
there is no hope that survives time.

I do not know this soldier, but his city is no more,
and the road that ran beside it, famous for camels
weighed down by trade, has ceased to exist.

History has moved with the griots who knew
it will always move, leaving an empty house
that overlooks the desert where a red dress still hangs
outside a window—a sign that someone waited for the soldier
as the city emptied people out of their houses,
someone whispered his name until they became a ghost.

A Train Stop in the Sahara

Who would have thought that man's hunger
for movement would lead him here? Perhaps
the ancient ones knew; they saw the journey,
man's endless desire for conquest.

And by the train stop, a journalist asked
the turbaned man about the desert's boredom,
its vast emptiness, gray skies. Do you feel
left out of the world, do you long to see the sea?

The man replied, the desert is my mother;
what she owns she hides from the world,
what she hides, she offers to those who know
her language. When I am asleep, she holds me.
When the train comes, I hold her, chanting,
this too shall pass. I have no need for the sea.
My world is underneath my feet; within it
there is an endless flow of water.

The turbaned man walked away from the train
stop. At his invitation I followed him. I envied
the vast nature of his home: the pot on a fire lighted
by desert shrubs, his axe coming down the spine
of a slain lamb, children napping under a tent,
women braiding hair, planning the night's feast.

I, nomad, who have walked through cities,
soundless like a bone thrown into a pit,
I have no language for belonging.

I have wished for nothing but this: let me live
outside the violence of time, let me watch
a passing train, listening as a turbaned man describes
his camel waiting by a wall, waiting for water.

My tenderness toward the turbaned man
was a form of longing, not meditation,
just pure hunger, the body asking,
now that I have touched your home,
can I walk through the lonely path
heading for home?

At the Edge of the Desert

for Chinguetti

In the Library of Sand, there are bookshelves
holding back the dead from leaving. The shadow
before a bill of sale, an old parchment stored
in a bamboo tube, belonged to a dead scholar
who once traveled along the Nile, saying
to boatmen on flatbottom boats, your people
are my people—so said the librarian who led us
through rows and rows of parchments.

Here, he said, a famous scholar once sat cross-legged
on a stool, studying deep into midnight while lizards
followed trails of boys who walked these courtyards,
barefooted, seeking parakeets gifted to them by pilgrims.

The reading rooms were filled with prayers,
with meditations of the dead, with voices
of tourists who had traveled from afar.

After praying I reflected on journeys,
all those who arrived at Chinguetti, stooping
so they could walk through library doors,
rising into the quiet of old places,
knowing what those who came before them
knew: we are all dumb to the world beyond our eyes.

At the end of our tour, the librarian,
who was also a tour guide, counted his earnings.
The parrots, inheritors of the parakeets' cages,

were empty of songs; the doors of history were closed
to us, and in the call to prayers was the warning,
let the dead read their writing, let the dead stay dead
on their altar of sands, in memories hidden in dust
covering books, in the calligraphy of their endless labor.

Mist

I entered a train station
and the air trembled, swallows searched
for rooms in the brief wonder of flight.

The graffiti on the pillars spoke of nothing.
The day ran into the night
like a child who having been harmed
by a stranger must seek refuge
in the darkness of a closed room.

I wanted the world to be still, the clouds
shaped like bicycles to stop moving.
I wanted the girl, whose black clothes spoke
of mourning, to look at me.

The world has happened, I had left home,
and from afar I could imagine the houses
on the hill of my birth, the houses leaning
into each other like old souls falling
into the slow embrace of pity.

The doors to my country have been closed
to me, the canvas of my mind torn into shreds.
What home I knew is now the abode of hawks,
and the falconer whose falcon escaped
into the wild must begin to think about freedom.

In every mirror, I said to myself, I did not die
today; the world kept moving.

At my departure I said goodbye, I said welcome,
I said nothing, and the city turned its back at me,
becoming a stranger I will walk past someday,
in a country beyond the river of mirrors.

The Gallery at the End of Time

after Ben Enwonwu's painting Tutu

It is pointless now: the old masters are gone,
their works stowed in the attic,
labeled carefully after the years of their brilliance,
and though I have tried to map the places
they walked through—Venice, Owerri, Botticelli's
Florence, and even the settlement in the desert
where decomposing bodies of shepherds
wrapped in cotton, old corals, bones of dead camels,
and cow horns have continued to sculpt, out of the earth,
a lesson in the abstract nature of life—I have failed
to witness the acrylic heaven, bounty of colors,
the gradual unveiling of marble. Tethered by my chain
to words, I walked and stood in front of every painting,
every sculpture, taking lessons in symmetry, expecting
to see through canvas an old man sitting before the Seine,
drawing with charcoal the last evening of a dying master.
In the middle of beauty, imagination failed me.
I have stood before Ben Enwonwu's long lost Tutu,
the sharp gaze of her eyes, her blue blouse
like the evening sky, and then under her chin
a subtle burst of light. Where does it lead?
When last did it light a face? There are
disappearances that are curated to hold us in wonder.
There are beautiful moments so powerful they give
grace unto darkness like these paintings, like my mother.
The gallery has been emptied, each work of art
taken away, each of them saying, before entering
their crates, *I have spent my time under the sun, so another*

may take my place. And beside me, an art critic wrote down
these words: *We may never see the likes of these again,*
the gradual flirting with light, the gradient, O beauty, O beauty.
I have not studied the history of all art, but having
witnessed the stampede of those who seek the peace
that comes out of holiness, I knew that perfection leads
to chaos, that love holds in its palm the balm of death
and eternity. And as I walked the night, knowing that out
of the darkness of time, a new school of old masters
were getting ready to know light again, I knew the lens
of the world was upon me. I smiled, waiting for my end,
for the light of the world to descend upon a poet
writing in a small room in St. Louis, reciting the poems
of Haji Gora Haji. O poet of reed and sea songs,
I have been traveling toward you, bringing
to your old city the darkness that I have become.

II. REMEMBRANCE

If I cast my eyes backward, to my homeland, I am accosted
with the horrors of history, the greed of men, the unspoken
terror. Yet, from afar I see the gaps, the hope, wonder. I see
all of our prayers and like a farmer waiting for a storm to pass,
bringing sunshine after it, I wait and write what must be written.
—Journal entry, August 16, 2018

From Darkness into Light

Once, at night, I saw the world collapsing
into a song. A man who has known loneliness
throughout the day was summoning all the voices
left outside doors to his side; his flute said:
God, do not begrudge me this hour of creation.
And God replied—there is nothing to begrudge,
for I was once lonely, staring at the dark,
and I said, let there be light, for I, too, was afraid
of the emptiness before me. I told this to the Reverend
who was called to pray for me, once after my stomach
was pumped and the drugs gone from my system,
once after I listened to a dying cockerel and asked
my mother, what lushness has death seen? What beauty hides
in its body that it invites the world, screaming into every house,
you must come into where the waters have been,
you must see the flowers, the swifts, the lizards, all bowing
and praising, all saying, it is through the earth
we become saved. And the Reverend said, you must be a savant,
not a poet, for who without school can sing the world
into verse? I have said nothing of this exchange, not to my lover,
who once over wine asked me, when did you become
a poet? Not to my mother, who said, do not choose to suffer.
Although once, beside a river where goats come to drink,
I said to the wild, it is only fair that those who hunger must cry,
it is only fair that those whom the world shaped
through pain must begin to cry into wind. And the wild replied,

you must not seek understanding, your language is extinct,
a dead thing wandering at the boundary of darkness; you must
hold it and shout, only language can begin the restoration
of those pushed out of history. I have been shouting into light.

In the Middle of August, I Saw the Sky

One morning, on a wet day during the week,
in which I had sharpened my cutlass from dark
till dawn, braving for the stubbornness of wet leaves,
for the wet branches of trees that grew across
the farm path, snatching at legs, saying in their quiet
voices, there is nowhere you can escape from life,
there is nowhere you can escape from the resurrection
of dead things.

Then, there was the wild that stood before me,
an old forest filled with the survivors of fallen trees,
where macabre monkeys called and responded,
and if one was lucky a big bird, with red and white plumage
like a cloth wrapped around the bruised body of the dead,
would fly by, saying nothing like the dead moving
from one life to another, migratory like the wild boar
who woke himself out of a grave.

Everything was a prelude to wonder.
The roots of trees gossiped different farmers,
mocking those whose crops have withered.
I sung the ballad of the river. Having crossed
the gully, I turned toward my farm—scarecrows
made out of my grandfather's clothes welcomed
me to the earth, and I welcomed the many dead,
those who walked in my shadow.

There was no time to finish the half work of nature.
So, I sat on a rotten log and viewed row after row
of young pineapples, all of them blossoming
like little eyes, watching me back, and I thought
of all the eyes that were there: the trees, the birds,
the seeds ready to break from their past like men
running away from an old city, the deer watching
me behind the safety of leaves, and the earth
itself, all of us watching the sky, waiting for rain,
or for the silence to teach us a lesson—some lesson
about faith. After a while it was all over. I picked up
my cutlass, cutting down the first weed, cutting
down the world, as the trees stared at the duty of man,
which was the duty of hands.

A Stranger in Aba

after the women's war of 1929

In the dying afternoon, the stereo was on,
the stockfish seller hummed to a song about the days
of women marching against colonial masters, sitting
on men, protesting with the nakedness of their bodies.

All my life I have lived in small towns,
marveling at rolling hills, grasses green and lush, bicycle bells
tinkling down hills. I have lived in the dark. I went to school
with just a foot inside the house of knowledge, where history
was a spinning atlas, not the lives of our people.

I didn't know who those women were,
what cities they left from, but on hearing that song,
I stopped and listened. The city, all concrete
and wild, stared me deep in the eyes. At the end,
I heard the voice of an old poet,

You will never know the depth of your history.
Do not be ashamed of your life; the birds are shameless in flight,
the woodpecker knows what we don't, so it spends its life writing to trees.
And down the overflowing stream, where little boys still cast their hooks,
fishes swim by with the prayer of survival: let water protect me from the hunger
of man, let the hand that pulls me out of my home be gentle in leading me back.

When I looked back, I saw myself in a mirror, old and still waiting
for knowledge—and down the road, ducks were passing through,
slowly living in the ecstasy of themselves.

Last Days of General Abacha

As for those who are dead there is nothing
we can do other than imagine them living
their lives under murky waters, in the canal
of Apapa. There is nothing like victory
in a dictatorship; those who survive must carry
within them the map of blood, the desire to find
missing bones. Perhaps we all carry within us
the illumination of knowledge—though we had
no choice but to say, this is where they were shot.

    And the days grew, though we wanted
no part of it. There was no strategy
that came out of our sorrow—that we mourned
also meant that we will forget.

I had walked away from the dead, afraid
to confront the air filled with words
upon words, filled with bronze wings
of angels, filled with their voices
calling into the canal, the void of their sorrow.

For a moment the world was as it wanted to be,
the turtles were home, the kingfisher was above water,
hunting the silver of a fish. From a pier a sailor
pissed into the sea. I wanted to stay there, to walk
beyond ripples into bazars of the north,

but the final history of the dead is that they are dead,
is that those alive must remember the last days
where a woman was heard wailing in the village
of our births. I have stood before her, hearing
her words. And now that I write in water,
I know there is no translation for our sorrow.
Still the boats will travel on them, ferrying those
who ran away from terror to where it all began.

Remembrance

after the Asaba Massacre

I won't tell the world to slow down.
Instead, I will say, come into my house,
sit, drink milk, and listen. I ran out,
I returned, and it was still the same picture
on my wall, still the same story spinning
in the waters of Asaba. The year running
back to 1967 when men clad in white were killed
like sacrificial doves while their mouths chanted,
One Nigeria! Years after their death,
I watched a man look into my eyes
without regret as he recounted the moment
the land covered its ears as bullets reduced sons
to silence. My mother said, some men don't feel
the pain of a dog passing away. I tried to tell her
that's what they were called as they marched them
to death, but she said, don't remember those things,
everyone has moved on, everyone has forgotten
the sound of men crying into the heart of God.
So, I ran to build a wall around my ears,
but their screams kept tearing it down. I ran
to take their names, the names of all who died
in the hands of a man that resembled a friend.
I listed them, and it was so long. I called;
no one answered. I walked into a house;
it was empty, the door unhinged.

On the walls were history, writings of cobwebs,
and beside old documents a mother buried
her wrinkled face into an old paper
as she searched for the name of her son.
I turned from her, and God felled.

Under the Mango Tree

The boys had their eyes dug out and were sent back to Biafra.
The boys were all about my age—twelve or thirteen—and even
the captain was only fifteen.
—*"Ben Okafor Remembers the Biafra War,"* BBC, *July 5, 2012*

That night will never be free. I was a boy hidden
underneath my father's shirt as he waded
through the flood. I saw the trees that grew
from skeletons buried on the darkest day of the war,
skeletons who were boys made to walk through villages
and markets blind—their bodies learning an ear could hear
a road. I touched the journal I held close to my chest
and wondered what history lived underneath
old brown leather as we waded past a church
whose stained-glass window trapped a boy-saint
yearning for light. I would have given up everything
to make that boy free. Sometimes, I listen to this story:
how Father kept me safe, wading until he saw
the mango tree and sang it to hide me, hoisting me
onto a tree branch. Some nights I wonder if those hands
made soft by music were the same hands that held a boy
during the war and shoved a bayonet in his eyes.
Or maybe those hands held the trumpet as sweet music
entered the air, the same time a boy called his father's name
to know mercy. I do know my history. This guilt knows me
well, but sometimes I listen to birds on my father's grave
and wonder if he knew some boy cried, *Captain! Captain!*
As a soldier rose to the anthem, spat out tobacco-filled saliva
into grasses shimmering with the blood of unanswered prayers,
with mothers' voices hiding in bunkers, with the wild grief of days.

Harmattan

for old soldier

And in December, when the roads were swept clean
by winds and the sky, absent of birds long gone,
reminded us of empty music halls, we walked
down the village. Past the police station
where a thief escaped from last night, scaling the fence
made out of twigs and broken bottles. There was a song
you wanted to sing, a song that began with a low hum,
an elegy for things not seen, a beginning that hoped
to save us from the past. But before you opened
your mouth another song entered the air,
leading you to silence. An old soldier who fought
in the civil war was humming the battles he fought, the days
spent cleaning his rifle, the days spent in a small airport
waiting to be airlifted. The moon was full,
a witness made to suffer through the night, throwing up
shadows. Not as a way of saying, I was there,
but a complaint made out of darkness and light,
a supplication to be left alone to beauty. I did not say
to you when we got home that the soldier was you
and the hum was you and the silence also.
That memory that you have held has known you too,
an anchor that's life giving and life taking, a road
that was lit up in battle and has refused to enter the dark.

The River Is by the Door

It is easy to wash the dead, the mortician said
as he stepped over bodies of the embalmed,
asking, *Where is your mother?* I was forced
there, dragged out of bed by my uncle
who is now dead, whose child also walked
my path, stepping over silence before pointing
a finger to his body, *Here lies my father*, the same way
I pointed to my mother's body, only I couldn't
say the words, so I was spoken for, redeemed
out of silence by the benevolence of strangers.
And the mortician asked, *Do you want her washed
or will you do it?* I followed the men who carried her
in a blanket, I watched them settle her on the veranda,
the afternoon was dead. Victor Uwaifo crooned
from a small radio. The market nearby erupted
into a chorus of life. I went down on my knees,
I washed her hands, her belly, I rubbed my hands
over the stiff cold body, tracing the lines
where the baby was taken out of her. Soap suds
pooled beside my legs, not going anywhere, like my anger,
like my sorrow. Why didn't the birds arrive?
The men watched me go down on my knees, I didn't cry,
I was worried the birds were dead too. *You are now a man*,
my uncle said. The world mirrored his words. I looked
at the soap suds, they erupted into her voice. It has been years,
sometimes I cry into the night, sometimes the night is heavy
with birds seeking redemption. I do not know how the dead

survive their new country, but the river outside my window
passes by, not stopping, not speaking. I want to ask
for knowledge, but I know why we don't allow parents
to witness the burial of their children, they have
no word for sorrow. The earth has no word for me.

Falling Dusk

And so it began, in the village of my birth;
those who longed for urban life
were nowhere to be found, their houses empty,

and chairs waited beside doors. These were little pieces
of remembrance on which their children once sat,
from which their children once listened
as the oldest man in the village reached for his raffia bag,
breaking kola nut before breaking a story out of himself.

I, too, have sat before him, listened as he spoke
about baobab trees, old spirits whose roots refused
to journey to distant pasts.

All of these are no more. Lost by years, the old man
who survived the war of long spears, capsized boats,
whose arthritic feet walked the streets every night,
recreating his journey to our village, was dying.

His eyes, filled with pus, could no longer see
the room where he once sat before a fire, crafting
stories from a spider's web.

I listened to him try to speak his language,
the one he dropped when he came here, picking up
our sounds. I listened as he, last of his water people,
laid down, murmuring to himself.

I would like to describe life, I would like to say,
on that bed, just before midnight, he looked at us,
young ones who came to say goodbye;
he opened his mouth, searching for a story,
dying just as a sound reached his tongue.

When I said to him *stay*, I knew it was the end.
When I said *we love you*, I knew I would speak
these words, sitting before a fallen house,
the baobabs too are going extinct, and someday
the old man's land, his voice, will call through the last tide
of a departing river. We will hear again the beginning of a story,
saying, the canoes made out of palm trees are under the shed,
and if you sail in one you will follow the path, sailing through
an old man's voice. O my heart—we who have witnessed
the death of language, what will become of us?

At Midnight I Dreamt of Rapture

The little bell at the end of our town
rang its truth: an ode to time,
an ode to the foolishness of life,
although at that time we didn't understand
it. Do not blame us, the absent children
of God. For how could we have known that
the end would arrive in its own solitude?

Even when marigolds spat out spores
of fairy angels, even when orange trees
embraced the bees, giving them rest,
even then, we didn't know the sky was tired
of itself. We were reading the papers, sorrowing
in the news of war, in the news of bamboos
cut down to make roads, in the last rites
and ceremony of someone we once knew.

How foolish were we to think that the earth
would stop and shout from treetops its last day,
that the cathedral built by the last ginger-haired
reverend from Ireland would shed its white paint
and become an anthill.

The world is the world, it hurries for no one.

And while we contemplated being left behind,
a messenger rode into town, blowing from his trumpet
another war. Down the road, from the house

whose fence had mermaids sculpted on it,
two lovers walked out the door, laughing
into moonlight. Yes, it is true, our world ended
in terror and in love. At last, which do I prefer?
I do not know. The world has passed over me,
and when I asked, what about my turn?
Not yet, it said, not yet.

Before the Arrival of Rain

Everything was the broad stroke of nature,
old light guided new light. Men set fire
to fallowed land, hawks glided over fleeing cane rats,
and just beyond the alfalfa, a family of bush dogs
ran into the wild, jumping over fallen trees.

Sitting at the border between burning land
and verdant green, a farmer and his son played
two flutes, eulogizing from the sky filled with ashes
the souls of those who died before the land
was ready to be plowed. At the end of the flutes'
eulogy the earth was ready to sprout yam vines—
there was rain, there was the end of bush fires,
there were dying embers of trees still standing,
thick stumps declaring that the brutal season
of rebirth had just begun.

And before stars mapped the night sky into old signs,
the farmer and his son walked the narrow road home,
thinking of clearing burnt land, for the tender nature
of planting is left to those who hold memories
of dead trees, tending in their calloused palms
the abundance of little seeds.

Every reincarnation begins this way,
every farmer's prayer begins this way:

may the dead find their path in the darkness of life,
may their rebirth be joyful, and when I touch
a young tree, may I remember when we were young,
when we held dried mango seeds, throwing them
until they hit a far wall and stopped, daring us to begin again.

The Gathering of Bastards

We are sailing toward Takwa Bay.
The light is waning. Fishermen offer prayers
to their faded nets, trusting what they can see.

I have no problem with God, although sometimes
I think about Noah's ark, all those animals walking
in pairs into loneliness.

Here, the sea mirrors the sky, a boat boy wolfs
down his dinner, and for some reason I think
we are closer to death. At the end, the island
welcomes us, all of us who were born
out of time, all of us who had walked across sand.

I do not trust time, or the welcome of strangers,
neither do I want to see the other side of light,
but the night is here,
water is flowing past the beginning of stones.

I do not trust what comes after the night sky,
after the resurrection of the sparrow's song,
but we are all laughing at the moon,
and in our quiet moment
when it feels like the world is learning again
how to speak, a boy whispers.
The sun is across water, it is daring us
to walk, calling the holiness of our names.

Waiting for Rain

*after the statues of men and women killed during the British
Massacre of Benin*

Driving past Ring Road, we see them,
the statues—men and women kissing into violence,
swords, spears, bayonets forgotten in their bodies
like the way time has forgotten the graves
of those who died in my childhood years,
whose innocence requires no headstone, no map,
for they fully belong to the earth. And the bats,
those messengers, are always flying above
the statues, saying to us in their wings
blanketing the sky, saying: these bodies
now sculpted before you stood against the White men,
these bodies were the first to fall, then the red walls,
then the city. Once when I was ten, a stranger
to this city, they came, the men, the women,
they came, saying: speak to us of the river
running through us, speak to us of trees,
and I said nothing, for what image is worthy
of the dead? Today, I know they will come again,
bringing with them the old smell of gunpowder, the smell
of mud, the wind weeping its uselessness to history.
I am not prepared to answer their questions,
I am not prepared to show them the poem I have written
since their last visit. And they will follow me,
all of them, like tin cans tied to a rope. They will scrape
the ground, their sound an ongoing mourning.
I am wedded to this fate of dusk and terror,
to this fate of rage and love. And before the night
comes I will walk down the riverbank; I will see

the rain. Yes, let my wet clothes hide my fear, let the time
come, let the river lead me to its bed, its country
filled with water plants, pebbles, castaways.
Let it hold me for a while, and when I come up
I will say to the dead: I was waiting for the rain.

At Lagos Polo Club

In the stalls where they held horses,
where a man in a red uniform once stood
in those years when the city was changing
and the sea, full of swift boats sailing
to offload crates of wine and butter,
was becoming a new language empty
of Guineamen; in the stalls where old British
officers once declared, *The sun will always shine
on our buttons and regalia,* a boy from my village
now mucks the forgotten hay. Sometimes he reads
the names of glorious horses who carried men
into fields. He tells me that in the silence of our halls,
where spirits feast at night to music, lies our past.
And I listen to him speak slowly into my left ear
the stories of colonial officers who rode the flesh
of both man and beast, who declared
through constitutions that we were half humans,
then full humans, then people who could read.
I listen and I sigh. I am birthed by blood to stories
of this city, to dark places that provide refuge,
to the marketplace where I, who was once homeless,
found a ground to lay my head. The umpire blows
his whistle, and the politicians, the new masters,
begin to ride into the field. We watch them
just as house boys belonging to colonial district officers
once watched their masters. As the men chase
after the bamboo ball, I look at a black horse,
I remember an old man saying, of those

whom the wind called in dreams the wild blood
of horses flows in them, leading to distant cities
of the reincarnated where house boys who were dead
are now strangers walking beside a movie theater,
whistling to themselves a country song full of blood.

III. WANDERER

I have lived within the margin of every city I arrived in,
an unacknowledged stranger. New to this despair,
I have gathered no riches, I yearned for no acclaim.
I, exiled poet and lover, desire rest. I desire the comfort
of my old mattress. O old friend, were you discarded
when I ran away or did you offer comfort to another?
—Journal entry, July 25, 2020

Assimilation

It was not the green of trees that welcomed
me to spring. It was not the resurrection
of dead fields that showed me that the way
through life could be green and tender.
It was a little dog, a terrier mix, running
around the park, yelping into the nothingness
of air, daring even God to stop her. I stood
for minutes outside the fence, watching her,
wondering about my life. In the Midwest
of America I have become domesticated
against the beauty of rainforests. Everything
has slowed down. The antelopes in my dreams
have stopped gliding over fallen logs; instead
they are strolling through the grasses, kept
out of the wild by a row of wooden fences
like I have been kept out of my country.
Is the end of my life the slowness of wonder?
I have forgotten the colony of bees,
I have forgotten the wild goats
chasing me on broken bridges as I ran
to drink sugar-filled coffee in roadside kiosks.
It is a thing of terror to stare into the lights
of your past, to fall to the ground, a broken being
trying to root his belonging into the depth
of a new world, becoming like a little dog
waiting for its first rain, starring at the clouds
with no knowledge of what it feels like
to surrender fear to the solitude of rainfall.

Asylee in the Evening of the World

At night when my gramophone wails
slowly the jazz of Ornette Coleman,
I wallow alone before the stars, surrounded
by my books like an elder before a circle
of children, like a storyteller pulling the strings
of the world.

I have wandered into the woods of an old poem
where cows run across a field, tinkling their bells.
Where the wind comes with remorse, and a farmer
watches the sky for the advent of rain.

On the bush path that leads to the village,
a woman whose son is lost in exile divines
from the blood of a chicken the life of a man
swallowed by the dusty corners of life.

The path descends, the wind finds songs
in the rustle of leaves, poco a poco, and in front
of the primary school, a van, filled with clowns
selling vanilla ice cream and cookies named
after St. Christopher, is parked on the football field.

No one knows the driver, although Joseph,
whom I once spent a night with in Bamako,
has stumbled out of a classroom, shouting
to the village, *Once you turn your back to a city,
the city turns its back at you!*

What you have lost will haunt you
in the darkness of your life,
what you have saved will desert you.

And under a tree, a boy, lost in the audience
of his soul, plays an accordion, leading me
to the village square where people have gathered
around an orange tree, debating the fate of a man
without a country.

I have known nothing of this life, or of fate.
I have walked into the world believing it will
accept me. As I step out of this poem, Ornette's
plastic saxophone sings the end of time.

O midnight of ghosts, the swallows are singing.
All arrivals are dead within me, all departures are birds
flinging their bodies against the cage of exile,
and I, a man without a home, must begin to write
of a lantern hooked on the roof of a departing train,
lighting the world ahead of refugees traveling to the shadow
of a new country.

The Migrant of Padua

for Johnbull

For those who have journeyed across the sea
love is not enough to declare home, and you
who have wandered during the day, taking
in the sight of lovers walking around Padua,
are awake at night, counting the many ways
a country can desert a man.

Under moonlight the roofs hold their own beauty,
and beyond streets catering to the silence of migrants,
Donatello's Gattamelata prepares to gallop
into battle. There is always, hiding in every city,
a forgotten story of violence.

And from the windows of Padua, the ghosts
of old women who witnessed the hanging of a noble
have also witnessed the migrant's shame—the lowering
of eyes by men who still beg for coins on street corners,
practicing Italian learned in refugee welcome centers,
saying, aiutami, ho fame. Help me, I am hungry.

Perhaps it is true that pigeons understand the ruthlessness
of these streets, performing their lives for bread.
And what is the performance of your life?
Exile? Old shoes? Slacked sweaters?
Or a father who after coming back from a hard day,
lifts his daughter to the sky, mapping
for her the wonder of his childhood?

Before the arrival of dawn, your clothes covered
with the splattering of blood, the aftermath
of a butcher's labor, hold you close. There is always
beauty existing beyond the suffering of our lives
like the birds twittering in the branches of a small tree,
like a man sailing a boat to the island of Capri.

And like the bull of your name, you have battled
with what is before you. You have left the doors open,
waiting for the end of suffering, for the arrival
of a prayer said in a quiet corner.

The world breathes to its own time, and we follow
in its wake. It is a lonely thing to admit,
but the brightness of this world requires its own sadness
like a refugee being welcomed by the sight
of a stranger drinking coffee while reading a novel
about the end of hunger,
the silent shattering of the world.

O Blue Waters, O Ships!

And though the day moved
into the entanglement of stars, and the moon
slowly opened itself, showing the orchestra
of faraway tides,

I chose to follow the movement of seagulls,
searching for a city without pain, called by old men
in the drinking shed, the foolishness of hope.

At every port the world unfolded itself
into the language of arrival—
sailors walked down gangways,
heavy with stories,
weighed down by the desire for fire.

The lowlands smelled of desperation,
gambling houses held the mud
of dreams. Red mangroves saw the anger
of lightning, burning their sorrow
into air, and though gray parrots repeated
words gleaned from the tongues of men
there was no emotion there.

Fate has fallen on me, the anchors have gotten old
and weary, and I have grown into the years of despair,
waiting for the sound of a new city to approach me.

On water, where every boat carries a prayer
against floundering, the paddles kept paddling the sea
for answers. It is September now, and in a distant port
another man is getting ready to step on a ship,
bringing aboard his odyssey. This world knows
us so well, the seabed is filled with dreams
sleeping in the dark, and between waves lies the city
of impatience. O be still, every date tree promises
the sweetness of the earth, and the world
we know is laughing into a new age; still

I look to the ships,
waiting for them to move swiftly like dolphins
swimming toward a rocky island
filled with horses, fabled to be paradise
by those who wept the end of Constantinople.

In the Museum of Fine Arts,
I Remembered Home

In the wake of my exile, the fish market blossomed
down the river. A child drove a toy car through the open veranda
of my childhood, and down the road, in front of every house,
there was a gutter where little fishes lived in their own world.
For four years, I have not spoken a word to the blood
of my home, although I have received mails,
saying the wheelbarrow boys still wear my shirts, card players
still say my name, and the women of Crimson Brothel
still shake their heads on passing my door, remembering nights
when we all ate roasted meat, drank whiskey, and said to ourselves,
the poor of the earth belong to the society of happy fellows.
I have not disappeared from my history, I have not forgotten
the gnats that hovered over the lantern, the meat seller reciting
an old incantation. Today, I walked down Huntington Avenue,
the night of renewal approached me, the moon was becoming
a lamp to my past, shadows around me grew into the map
of a country. Everywhere I went held a stolen part
of my forebears; even the museum was filled with my disgrace.
For no reason, the crows came down from the birch tree
before me, starring into darkness. What evil has befallen
me has befallen those ahead of me, throwing them out
of their countries. So, I prayed in the language of winds,
as sincere as a whisper going out on water, let me touch
my forehead on the doorpost of my home. And here,
tonight, in Boston, the air is alive with the souls
of dead exiles, the sky too, and the dodo bird
that sings in our faraway land is watching me, singing
the folktale of rivers waiting for the souls of lost boats.

All Winter I Had No Love

though there was the frozen lake
I walked around three times every day
like a faithful pilgrim who had stumbled
upon a saint's grave and in that shock
of worship was unable to let go. All day
I thought of prayers and then discarded
them. The world itself was becoming small.
I stood on a balcony in Athens, looking at the bronze
of a racehorse, the raised point of its nostrils
still filled with smoke. I have seen every beauty
from the loneliness of my heart. I have walked
in dreams into a market in Ouagadougou,
and on a street where a French house was falling
apart, haggled with a woman for the bleached skull
of a wild hog. I had no use of it except to understand
what becomes of us when we are left alone.
Still alone, I said to myself, there is nothing
as familiar as cruelty—even exile, even love understands
its shadow. And in a garden of light, among snow men,
a little plastic Jesus blossomed into the night like tenderness,
like a stalk of wheat forgotten by time, and I plucked it.
Walking home, I imagined angel after angel traveling beside me,
and from above there was a song. I have known joy
only to suffer when it's gone. I have seen the hawk
circling the sky, seeking for the end of its hunger,
and though my soul was frail, I kept walking toward the end,
toward the house where my desire kept the walls warm.

Walking along Harvard Square

for Nadia, whose parents came from Senegal, child of exile and hope

We met at a junction;
                    from your face I could see
the drummers skinning a goat,
                    their tender hands holding the fur,
the gentle pull of skin from flesh
                    creating music that would bless a drum,
soft sounds escaping their throats
                    as prayers for the dead.
I do not know if you saw me;
                    I could hear the talking drum
in your footfalls.
                    The pom-poms peeking out of your bag,

perhaps a gift to your daughter, reminded me
                    of raffia roofs
from a village founded along a creek.

You, descendant of ritual drums and trumpets,
                    are African as I could ever be,
and as American as I could never be.

There was something in your footsteps,
                    in the song you whistled as you walked
that said you knew the lives of all there is.
                    In Jamaica Plain you would be home
on a sofa
in the presence of Doondari and the Court of Heaven.

You who whistled a thousand sparrows,
you knew your place

in the songs of praise, in the rituals of hills.
As you stepped into a car, I whistled
                    the song that passed from your being;
you stopped and saw me
                    under a streetlamp
as what stood on the shore.
                    I tried to speak as you walked toward me,
but you held my hand.

Now that we have known of each other,
                    what are we going to do?

Flyway

There is no light that holds the dead
in beauty like the light before nightfall,
that evening abundance of grace
luring the wild geese to stop on their way
to Mexico, bringing all that is gone
into a moment of homecoming.
I had walked through it once.
It was December, the cold was beginning,
and here in Ames, Africans at the crossroad
of life, refugees and migrants, were getting
ready to meet at a makeshift bar assembled
in a basement and named after a famous donkey
in Khartoum, so they said, where the rhumba
would wild out of speakers and we would seek
what those at crossroads seek: touch and joy,
sight and the safety of bodies. I had taken
my time before getting on the bus heading
to the bar. Walking down Coconino,
the dogs were out, blades of grass faded,
man-made lakes were filled with geese like airports
on water. Even in the midst of so much beauty
there is no place that will save us. Our destination
is between suffering and joy; everything else is a road
filled with unending patience. And even I, a nomad,
who have witnessed so much of the world,
will be forgotten before I reach the veranda
of my homeland. And yet as I watched the last light

of evening, waiting for the bus, I saw them, the dead,
descending on wings, joining the birds to play
in water, laughing into joy, and then they were gone.
All that was left was the only freedom we could speak
without shame, the weather, winter, the harmony of all things.

Atlantic Beach

I

Here, the mind wanders, gazing over the skin
of water. And all around me surfers yearn
for the wildness of waves just like when we walked
into rain, yearning to be led home, the world
and its voices falling down on us.

II

The coastline goes on and on, and a ship sits
on its own, lonely in water, like a forgotten toy
tossed into the sea. Everything before me
is blue and surgical, even the laughter of lovers.

III

My soul doesn't understand this world;
it walks on empty boulevards, and if you meet it
on a Sunday when the church that borders
the gas station erupts in holiness, perhaps it will say
to you, it is a terrible thing to be alive,
the world would do better with our silence.

IV

Beloved, sea gulls are diving out of the sky,
slowly becoming what comes out of dreams.
And from the umbrella of lovers, two dogs
are running into the sea; they do not hear

the whistle of their walkers—having gone mad
in the summer heat the dogs do what we all do,
they seek the calmness of water.

V

I have not given up on love.
Knowing the world is full of sadness
I have kept it in the silence of my pocket
and walked into the night.

VI

Here, the lanterns are out,
the night belongs to a wanderer,
the wounded whales are still out
there, seeking home.

And I, who was pronounced mad,
run into water, wondering what the lost wonder:
will the world end or will some majestic being
throw us into the wasteland of stars?

On Belonging

Again, to decolonize water is to walk into the sacredness
of rituals, meeting my mother, the long line of women
in white, all of them chanting, *Water will always lead us home.*

Once, I thought of Mali as paradise, all the griots
weaving stories into their genes, passing them down
from one generation to the other, but from
my veranda the world has shown me the missing
parts of my faith, all those succession battles,
those schemes behind the veil—the lineage of those
who were slaves, whose hands dug the gold
that followed the pilgrimage of Mansa Musa.

If the past had met us halfway into history,
perhaps it would say, *What I have to offer
is the succor of knowledge.* There is nothing
that war has not touched, even the leaves
still remember the weight of blood.

San Juan

I

The hour was upon us—all those bodies
jogging down the road, seeking perfection.

That morning, tenderness called.
Down the road, on the bridge,
an old man rested on an iron rail.
From his purse he threw into the canal
fish food after fish food, and the turtles
swam to him, fishes too,
and the swan that was visiting.

I turned away and continued the labor
of my life—the hard nature of the day
welcomed me, even the streets that staggered
out of the sea, even the man that played
a guitar on the grave of a dead soldier.
I was alive in the center of the world,
and when I turned back to look at tenderness
he was still there, singing calmly to departing turtles.

II

I have walked to the ocean's end, the spot
where the footsteps of God created a crater
of blue after blue wonder, where the birds
that surrounded me flew to the earth's desire,
migrating toward the promise of paradise.

I have walked into where the mourning of dolphins
led to an eternal song under water, where the fishes,
the whales, and the stingrays wandered into, eager
to understand what survives after the violence of creation.

This morning it rained; flowers blossomed into the path
of beauty. On my balcony I waited for water to fill me,
to wash out the debris of my soul. My body listened
to waves, to the death echo of my father, the gentleness
that remained after the wake of hurricanes.

Around my apartment lay the jagged edge of rocks,
places where the world broke us, then moved across
the ocean, leaving behind the afterthought of God,

the loneliness of grief. And in water, flamingoes lowered
their necks to the surrender of air. The men who waded
in the sea to remind themselves of the openness of life
have hurried home to their wives, leaving me to witness

the waves tumbling toward the shore of another country.
I am always at the border of things, always
at the spot where what returns is the fullness of hope.

I have prayed to walk down dusty roads with grace
by my side. I have lowered myself down the garden
of blood, and beside grape vines, where holiness
was empty, the finches, released from captivity,
swelled the air with songs. Alone and happy,
I waited for the shadow of God to pass me by.

A Man of Good Fortune

after Kwame Dawes

Clearly, the rhythm of my life lives in the night,
on the island where the movement of clouds
mirrors the movement of boats.

For days the city, where I now find myself,
was before me. In Porter Square, a man,
who was a stranger, looked at the movement
of the world, bringing out his saxophone
to play a song I last heard in Brass, sitting
just beyond the rhythm of the Atlantic.

I crouched in his shadow, wondering
how his music maps the journey of my life.
From his song I dreamt about the island,
the smell of sweat, the weaver of clothes
that sat before an old loom, weaving folktales
and cotton into a shirt I will wear someday.

On the scattered face of the earth, I searched
among the many radio stations, among the telescopes
mounted on the mountains of old ghosts.
The source of my pain was so precise, so small,
yet so great like a toothache worn deep into time,
like a country sailing away from a man.

In my little room, the tender memories of mercy
have found me, a reminder that I was once a young boy
standing in an assembly line, filled with innocence,

where we prayed the lord's prayer. I have wondered
about the path of my life—it is strange that in a faraway
land, in this place that asks about the origin of strangers,
I have found myself writing poems again.

I have arrived at the intersection of belonging,
the rats feed on the waste of us all, and I,
who must contend with the past, have brought
out the old gong. I, town crier and master of my fate,
I must beat my life into the existence of grace.

O master wind, little whisper of God,
tonight, I am writing to Brass. Lead me
over the wildness of waves, over the pulse
of the sea, and when I arrive at the sands
of progeny, let me witness those who arrived
in boats, who arrived with heavy clouds.

Let me witness their homecoming,
and if you so will, lead me to the fallen
house of my mother, to the altar
of my lineage washed with native chalk,
where the sea has come to worship the land,
where the dead and the living sing
of joy, breathing the fragrance of water.

Before Nightfall

Even this late, I imagine the goose,
whose partner is dead, dipping his head into water
to understand loss. I had hoped this wouldn't be me,

but here I am, watching the spires of buildings,
watching bicycles along a trail, children throwing Frisbees
at each other. I dip my toe into the coldness of a lake,
searching for a way back to my homeland.

And across the clarity of water, old regrets spill
themselves across the sky of Ames, bringing
with them a funeral—the fortieth day of mourning,
musicians playing outside a house, flowers
upon flowers, and a long line of women walking
around my old city, tracing every footstep
the dead took on earth.

I have not forgotten this belonging, this iridescent way
to death where burial is a way to claim ownership
of a body. Languishing in exile, I have been denied
passage to the foot of the dead, to the memorial
of my grandmother covered in white—the purity
of her age, the sum of time departing old bones.

The bereaved goose flies to meet his flock.
As I watch them go, a comet passes through
the clouds, opening this world to another
where candles light themselves as if in a sacred ritual
and water reflects to us our idea of beauty.

The earth is merciful in the passage of time.
Tonight, I will sleep on the couch again,
the silence will throb, and out of darkness
butterflies will bloom, asking for nothing
special, just the turning of time,
a transition so radiant it is visible to God.

Solstice

for Mayowa Coker

So, this was what happened on your last day here:
a blemished heron stood on the riverbank waiting;
the stone it stood on said in a quiet voice,
It has been hours, there are no fish in the water,
I am tired of carrying your hunger.
The river moved and moved, laughing
in the way water could, lapping
every stone on its borders. The sky laughed
also, saying to the stone, *Be patient,*
give thanks to the sun polishing you
each day, give thanks to every little rain.
I have carried your silent prayers
for decades, so you may carry for a little while
the animal crying for blood. I knew you
would have listened to these conversations
in their thousand languages, saying to each animal
lounging in the shades of trees, there is no hunger
that is endless, there is no joy that is infinite,
when we close the door to God, the door to heaven
will open a thousand times and in its endless light
we will travel. How could I have known
that your hunger was over? You are no more,
and on the day in which the city I lived in
was farther from the sun, I walked miles
into the woods held hostage by ice, saying
in that wise voice of yours, the dead shall spend
their last day on earth wandering around
their houses. They shall travel well into the sun,

and when the light finds them, I will,
in the aloneness of my being, wave to those
who have become tails of brilliant fires. Sometimes
we carry death, sometimes death carries us,
and you who have chosen to ride the night
will light the river, setting aflame your departure.

A Phone Call from Exile

I remember your face, veteran
of the Mediterranean, of sea crossings,
veteran of boats. I listen in stillness.

I do not say to you, my guilt is America.
I listen to you talk of shurroty, the act of begging
for food in an Italian city, the disappointment of exile.

What duty is asked of me other than to witness,
other than the uselessness of my craft?

Quiet like days after the defeat
of freedom, I go in to my room;
my plants mock me in their splendor.

Once when we were little, shielded from the brutal
realities of roads, we walked the woods, singing to birds,
playing on concrete verandas. You said the world
welcomes all to its journey. And we have walked,

and we have walked, and now you call again;
I, who am ashamed of my comfort,
do not answer. Weeping
into plants, I say, grow in my shame.

It is nighttime and I must go to sleep
wondering what refugee camp you will sleep in
tonight, what ancestor will lie at your feet.
I do not pray for you, I do not pray for me,
I only lie in my shame, I only bid sleep come.

Nomad

In Brooklyn, we drink to a toast
in Samar's asylum, seeking how to quiet
the countries speaking in our mouths.

There is no memory whole enough to gather joy
into our eyes, into nights when we stayed awake
crying for what we've lost, souls standing

at crossroads. The road has led to roads
that lead to other roads, and on this journey
I have become a creature devoted to water.

You will know us, nomads, by our thirst,
by the way we love—creating new worlds
in a strange land, rearranging tongues,
quaking history.

Now I say, my country is my desire,
every water I speak to knows my soul,
every road yearns to take me back.

I am in the dust of existence, in the exiled
song of water, in the flow of rivers.
How quick I embrace the world,
then lose it. The body is history,
a relic at work. Every river is a journey,

and I have gone along, a pebble skipping
through water. Where I sink will be home,
alive in the language of exiled cartographers,
in maps seeking the way of water, alive in a mother
still waiting for a son at the crossroads.

Full Moon

Lost in the desert, the Tuareg read the sky,
said, *No map is as beautiful as the stars.*

It has been years since I sat on cold sands,
watching camels, watching hookah smoke
rise into the sky's darkness.

Earlier this evening, the butcher
at Krokrobite washed away blood
from the counter. Kids on seesaws
jumped from one life to another.
And in roadside restaurants, lovers
read food menus with glee in their eyes.

Even in peace, I watched the world
from my window. Here, in my little room,
plants are dying, my mother's photograph
frowns at my burning cigarette.

I admit, I have learnt how to obey
the past. I keep nothing, I own nothing.
My bag, black, is beside my bed. Beside darkness
lies my little pouch of stars. The night cares
only for lovers. When I leave, I was never here.

Isla Verde

Here, where children sang "Vete," where we ate roasted
pork by the roadside, water has returned to calmness.

On the beach, men with red coolers are selling beers.
I walk down the road; people after Hurricane Maria
are trapped in the aftermath of hope.

Beside the bend, a house sold cheaply to developers
reminds land of its gaping wound. I sit on a window;
sorrow stays with me.

A song drifts from the beach; a man sings of owning
nothing. How same is the tenor of suffering, how alive
is my country in songs, in exile.

Under the sky, I smoke, thinking of aunties, of cheap calls
across the sea, of the women, loud and graceful, dancing
revival on sands.

In the blue evening, tourists paraglide back to land.
Lights and beauty of Marriott's Garden hold parties.

Here, where flower-patterned shirts hold memories
of the slave trade, I keep quiet, complicit by blood,

footprints left by Black traders on West Africa's
shore. The ancestors sold to ships are here, all eager,
all defeated. Silent in history, silent now, all my life
the sea was waiting to be written.

Lamentation

for Olokun

Because my legs have traveled
to far places, I must sing
with the iron bell. Your praises
are the mist of morning. The river
full of mirrors is not enough
to show your beauty.
O what remorse is at my doorstep?
Will the ocean recognize me?
My song bows, who will raise it?
Who will sing when the flash
of your skirt lifts the fishes?
Every deity becomes small
in translation, and I, who am to you
a son, am adrift. Where do I run to
when the ritual of my life becomes
undone? Where do I pray? The jiggle
of the Priestess' feet is lost to wind,
foamy waves are without cowries.
Without song there is silence,
eternal. Where do I go from here?

Offerings

for Lolo, who died at sea

In the dream that leads me back home, I am on the coast
of Malta. Around me migrant ghosts in shipwrecks echo

the night. I dive into water knowing the communion
of the drowned awaits me.

In water I bid farewell to my brother, he who saw me
hungry and fed me, not food but spirit, and I whispered,
Love, love, love, all over our city.

Allow me to bring back from water the memory
of the dead, to bring back the pendant on his neck,
the dead skull of my beloved still waiting for rescue,
his eyes still filled with stories they wait to tell
friends in a café outside of Florence
where Black boys who can't speak Italian gather
in the evening, begging for coins, shouting
shurroty, not knowing its meaning
other than I am starving outside of language.

In the darkness of water, I am alive,
a being in harmony with those who know
the agony of leaving home. And I say to my brother,
let us go together into the afterlife, down halls
where we lived in the past, where we saw each other
before going our separate ways, him to the desert
that leads to sea, I to America, where my survival
taunts me, a nightmare waiting at the edge
of every city, a knife in the room of sleep.

Ode to Shadows

for Igue festival

All around, our lives
beholden to tradition waited
for new year's gates to be opened.

At the palace, chiefs danced to the death
of the old year. Pigeons, released, sliced air
with wings to celebrate the triumph of joy.

Trapped in memories passed down,
the priest called on light.

At the end, palace gates emptied our joy
into streets of our births. The sun, tired
of our dance, slept into the night.

Across the ocean, in Iowa, I was trapped
in a park, waiting for dawn. O how alive
are memories of joy, how swift. The pigeons
are here, on the park bench, tap dancing.

Echoes

In Boston, I walked the night.
From blackness I beheld the salvation
of dreams. I have moved.

In rural Oregon, the plants spoke.
Red alders, white oaks stood still.
Two geldings ran around
in a small enclosure,

tiny creatures ran underneath
my foot as I walked the wooden bridge
that separated a small pond
from paths leading to a farmhouse.

So much hope ran through this familiar
space. Across the bridge I saw the algae
of my childhood. I trembled, I fell
to the ground, it was August.

I heard the earthworms saying,
We are of this world.
This world is ours only,
our great bounty, in it you live.

In all your yearning for home,
you can only tread this pond
from here to there, the beginning
of a narrowing path.

The Revolution Is Over

And if I come to you there will be no mountain
between us. I will not hide in an uncompleted building
with walls covered with algae. I will hear the young
speak to the man on the podium, our leader who slept
as army trucks rolled into Lagos, killing those
who woke the night in protest. I have no patience
for the language of cities, I was never raised in one;
a proper child of roads, I was given nothing,
I wanted nothing. There is no good that comes out
of consciousness, only pain, the awareness that many
will sleep hungry tonight and those whose graves
testify against policemen will wake in us. And if I come
to you, it is to witness chaos; there will be no peace
on the television, a revolution will walk the streets,
the traffic warden will wave it through, the women
will chant as it runs through muddy roads.
And if I come to you there will be a gun in my hand.
I, a coward, whose poems have taken root in another
country, what can I offer to blood, to those whose morning
is sorrow? I left the country and the country left me;
from afar I saw history get out of a broken-down bus,
I saw the young hold its hand. Do not mention my name,
I hopped on a plane and took to the skies. The days have gone,
the months are here, the man who lives in my mirror
is no more. The revolution is over, the roads have been cleared,
the burning toll gates quenched. And if I come to you
there will be a gun in my hand, there will be no one
beside me. I have become a poet of the past; what is there
to say, what will the fates be, what fire burns without me?

Returnee

I might have seen in the mist
the boatman sailing into the sea's blindness
as a prayer leaves his mouth slowly,
solemnly, into a God we cannot see.

I might have seen the sea's grace,
the way it returns the drowned
to be buried in the cemetery,
underneath the iroko tree
that borders the Street of Saints.

I might have seen the woman who fries fishes
in an old skillet, whose shadow is part
of the process, a time-honored tradition
to women who sat there,
in that market, frying and singing.

I might have seen the nets, old and worn,
yet still heavy with the faith of a fisherman
who spent all night mending holes,
whose son held a lantern as he worked,
the same way he once held a lantern
as his father sewed the nets,
watching the path of restoration.

To return to the present is to return
to the past, is to be shed of exile,
the worry of roads, before entering the dust

of belonging—the village with brown roofs,
the streets where children run half-naked,
diving into the sea. I claim this return,
I claim this sea, I claim this village,
and with it I claim the cemetery and the sky
above it, that patch of darkness and stars,
that place of hope that says, this land, loamy
and full of our dead, will one day heave for us.

Salute from the Boston Cold

Thinking of my beloved city,
I imagine a flock of birds
taking to the sky, heading
to the origin of their lives.

My hands have forgotten
the walls of our houses, the sound
of afrobeats from the roadside.

Lost to me are shrines of my birth,
our survival of the Royal Trading Company,
history of fights with Britain, with ships,
with those who came with the weather,
rising and falling.

There is thirst from exile;
rivers have become ice-skating rinks.

O the crippling thirst of home,
the songs I can no longer sing.
Desire sung into a void is still desire,
and I am left to witness the plunder of self.

Once in a movie, I watched
an actor return to his homeland,
his legs gone. I wept on my way
home. On the train, strangers were staring
at me. In the midst of it all

I was yearning for freedom
like a bird rattling against the cage
of his life, singing nothing, demanding
neither grain nor water,
just the open air, the skies, then death.

Eight New-Generation African Poets:
A Chapbook Box Set
Edited by Kwame Dawes
and Chris Abani
(Akashic Books)

New-Generation African Poets:
A Chapbook Box Set (Tatu)
Edited by Kwame Dawes
and Chris Abani
(Akashic Books)

New-Generation African Poets:
A Chapbook Box Set (Nne)
Edited by Kwame Dawes
and Chris Abani
(Akashic Books)

New-Generation African Poets:
A Chapbook Box Set (Tano)
Edited by Kwame Dawes
and Chris Abani
(Akashic Books)

New-Generation African Poets:
A Chapbook Box Set (Sita)
Edited by Kwame Dawes
and Chris Abani
(Akashic Books)

New-Generation African Poets:
A Chapbook Box Set (Saba)
Edited by Kwame Dawes
and Chris Abani
(Akashic Books)

New-Generation African Poets:
A Chapbook Box Set (Nane)
Edited by Kwame Dawes
and Chris Abani
(Akashic Books)

To order or obtain more information on these or other University of
Nebraska Press titles, visit nebraskapress.unl.edu. For more information
about the African Poetry Book Series, visit africanpoetrybf.unl.edu.

Printed in the USA
CPSIA information can be obtained
at www.ICGtesting.com
LVHW041146151223
766480LV00002B/230